2017 SQA Past Papers with Answers

Higher
BUSINESS MANAGEMENT

2014 Specimen Question Paper,
2015, 2016 & 2017 Exams

HODDER
GIBSON
AN HACHETTE UK COMPANY

This book contains the official 2014 SQA Specimen Question Paper, 2015, 2016 and 2017 Exams for Higher Business Management, with associated SQA-approved answers modified from the official marking instructions that accompany the paper.

In addition the book contains study skills advice. This advice has been specially commissioned by Hodder Gibson, and has been written by experienced senior teachers and examiners in line with the Higher for CfE syllabus and assessment outlines. This is not SQA material but has been devised to provide further guidance for Higher examinations.

Hodder Gibson is grateful to the copyright holders, as credited on the final page of the Answer section, for permission to use their material. Every effort has been made to trace the copyright holders and to obtain their permission for the use of copyright material. Hodder Gibson will be happy to receive information allowing us to rectify any error or omission in future editions.

Hachette UK's policy is to use papers that are natural, renewable and recyclable products and made from wood grown in sustainable forests. The logging and manufacturing processes are expected to conform to the environmental regulations of the country of origin.

Orders: please contact Bookpoint Ltd, 130 Park Drive, Milton Park, Abingdon, Oxon OX14 4SE. Telephone: (44) 01235 827720. Fax: (44) 01235 400454. Lines are open 9.00–5.00, Monday to Saturday, with a 24-hour message answering service. Visit our website at www.hoddereducation.co.uk. Hodder Gibson can be contacted direct on: Tel: 0141 333 4650; Fax: 0141 404 8188; email: hoddergibson@hodder.co.uk

This collection first published in 2017 by
Hodder Gibson, an imprint of Hodder Education,
An Hachette UK Company
211 St Vincent Street
Glasgow G2 5QY

Typeset by Aptara, Inc.

Printed in the UK.

A catalogue record for this title is available from the British Library.

ISBN: 978-1-5104-2143-1

2 1

2018 2017

Introduction

Study Skills – what you need to know to pass exams!

Pause for thought

Many students might skip quickly through a page like this. After all, we all know how to revise. Do you really though?

Think about this:

"IF YOU ALWAYS DO WHAT YOU ALWAYS DO, YOU WILL ALWAYS GET WHAT YOU HAVE ALWAYS GOT."

Do you like the grades you get? Do you want to do better? If you get full marks in your assessment, then that's great! Change nothing! This section is just to help you get that little bit better than you already are.

There are two main parts to the advice on offer here. The first part highlights fairly obvious things but which are also very important. The second part makes suggestions about revision that you might not have thought about but which WILL help you.

Part 1

DOH! It's so obvious but …

Start revising in good time

Don't leave it until the last minute – this will make you panic.

Make a revision timetable that sets out work time AND play time.

Sleep and eat!

Obvious really, and very helpful. Avoid arguments or stressful things too – even games that wind you up. You need to be fit, awake and focused!

Know your place!

Make sure you know exactly **WHEN and WHERE** your exams are.

Know your enemy!

Make sure you know what to expect in the exam.

How is the paper structured?

How much time is there for each question?

What types of question are involved?

Which topics seem to come up time and time again?

Which topics are your strongest and which are your weakest?

Are all topics compulsory or are there choices?

Learn by DOING!

There is no substitute for past papers and practice papers – they are simply essential! Tackling this collection of papers and answers is exactly the right thing to be doing as your exams approach.

Part 2

People learn in different ways. Some like low light, some bright. Some like early morning, some like evening / night. Some prefer warm, some prefer cold. But everyone uses their BRAIN and the brain works when it is active. Passive learning – sitting gazing at notes – is the most INEFFICIENT way to learn anything. Below you will find tips and ideas for making your revision more effective and maybe even more enjoyable. What follows gets your brain active, and active learning works!

Activity 1 – Stop and review

Step 1

When you have done no more than 5 minutes of revision reading STOP!

Step 2

Write a heading in your own words which sums up the topic you have been revising.

Step 3

Write a summary of what you have revised in no more than two sentences. Don't fool yourself by saying, "I know it, but I cannot put it into words". That just means you don't know it well enough. If you cannot write your summary, revise that section again, knowing that you must write a summary at the end of it. Many of you will have notebooks full of blue/black ink writing. Many of the pages will not be especially attractive or memorable so try to liven them up a bit with colour as you are reviewing and rewriting. **This is a great memory aid, and memory is the most important thing.**

Activity 2 – Use technology!

Why should everything be written down? Have you thought about "mental" maps, diagrams, cartoons and colour to help you learn? And rather than write down notes, why not record your revision material?

What about having a text message revision session with friends? Keep in touch with them to find out how and what they are revising and share ideas and questions.

Why not make a video diary where you tell the camera what you are doing, what you think you have learned and what you still have to do? No one has to see or hear it, but the process of having to organise your thoughts in a formal way to explain something is a very important learning practice.

Be sure to make use of electronic files. You could begin to summarise your class notes. Your typing might be slow, but it will get faster and the typed notes will be easier to read than the scribbles in your class notes. Try to add different fonts and colours to make your work stand out. You can easily Google relevant pictures, cartoons and diagrams which you can copy and paste to make your work more attractive and **MEMORABLE**.

Activity 3 – This is it. Do this and you will know lots!

Step 1

In this task you must be very honest with yourself! Find the SQA syllabus for your subject (www.sqa.org.uk). Look at how it is broken down into main topics called MANDATORY knowledge. That means stuff you MUST know.

Step 2

BEFORE you do ANY revision on this topic, write a list of everything that you already know about the subject. It might be quite a long list but you only need to write it once. It shows you all the information that is already in your long-term memory so you know what parts you do not need to revise!

Step 3

Pick a chapter or section from your book or revision notes. Choose a fairly large section or a whole chapter to get the most out of this activity.

With a buddy, use Skype, Facetime, Twitter or any other communication you have, to play the game "If this is the answer, what is the question?". For example, if you are revising Geography and the answer you provide is "meander", your buddy would have to make up a question like "What is the word that describes a feature of a river where it flows slowly and bends often from side to side?".

Make up 10 "answers" based on the content of the chapter or section you are using. Give this to your buddy to solve while you solve theirs.

Step 4

Construct a wordsearch of at least 10 × 10 squares. You can make it as big as you like but keep it realistic. Work together with a group of friends. Many apps allow you to make wordsearch puzzles online. The words and phrases can go in any direction and phrases can be split. Your puzzle must only contain facts linked to the topic you are revising. Your task is to find 10 bits of information to hide in your puzzle, but you must not repeat information that you used in Step 3. DO NOT show where the words are. Fill up empty squares with random letters. Remember to keep a note of where your answers are hidden but do not show your friends. When you have a complete puzzle, exchange it with a friend to solve each other's puzzle.

Step 5

Now make up 10 questions (not "answers" this time) based on the same chapter used in the previous two tasks. Again, you must find NEW information that you have not yet used. Now it's getting hard to find that new information! Again, give your questions to a friend to answer.

Step 6

As you have been doing the puzzles, your brain has been actively searching for new information. Now write a NEW LIST that contains only the new information you have discovered when doing the puzzles. Your new list is the one to look at repeatedly for short bursts over the next few days. Try to remember more and more of it without looking at it. After a few days, you should be able to add words from your second list to your first list as you increase the information in your long-term memory.

FINALLY! Be inspired...

Make a list of different revision ideas and beside each one write **THINGS I HAVE** tried, **THINGS I WILL** try and **THINGS I MIGHT** try. Don't be scared of trying something new.

And remember – "FAIL TO PREPARE AND PREPARE TO FAIL!"

Higher Business Management

The exams

It is important for you to be aware that in the examination paper **there is no choice of questions**. The structure of the examination is outlined below.

Section one

This is based on a case study of approximately 700 words and it will include additional information in the form of exhibits (appendices). The exhibits could include financial information, graphs or charts, pictorial information, timelines etc.

This will be followed by a total of 30 marks' worth of questions. Most of the questions will relate to information contained in the case study and exhibits, and may make reference to that information. It is important that your answers to the questions relate back to the information in the case study and exhibits. There will be a maximum of around eight questions which may be split into parts. The questions can be drawn from any area of the course and will use a variety of different command words. The aim of this section of the paper is to test breadth of knowledge from any part of the course.

Section two

This section of the examination paper is made up of four questions worth 10 marks each. The 10 marks will be split into a maximum of three parts in most cases, although you may see some questions split into just two parts. The aim of this section of the paper is to test depth of knowledge and each 10-mark question will focus on one topic area of the course. The questions can be drawn from any area of the course and will use a variety of different command words.

The main topic areas of the course, which you should already know, that are available to test are:

1. Understanding business
2. Management of people
3. Management of finance
4. Management of marketing
5. Management of operations

Whilst areas 2, 3, 4 and 5 are fairly equally weighted, area 1 is large in comparison so it is fair to expect to be asked statistically more questions from this area of the course.

Answering questions in Higher Business Management

Read the question carefully

It is often easy to assume you know what you are being asked in a question by picking out a few keywords. You will be in a high-pressure situation whether you think you are or not, and it's easy to try and get through the paper quickly.

Take the time you need to read the question carefully. It is essential that you answer the question being asked in order to maximise the number of marks that you can access. No question is deliberately worded to catch you out, or be a test of English, but you do need to understand how and why command words are used.

For example, "Describe the role of managers in staff appraisals" caused problems for many candidates as they either described the role of the manager or staff appraisals. This did not answer the question and so they could not be given marks. The role of manager had to be *related* to staff appraisals in order to answer the question fully and correctly.

Answering the command words

Each question in Higher Business Management has a command word to help you understand what is needed in your response. Some of the most common command words used are listed below with an explanation of what is required in your response. This list is not exhaustive and other command words could be used. Typically, in the Higher Business Management examination papers, "describe" is the most commonly used command, while the command which causes candidates the most problems (possibly because it demands more knowledge and application of that knowledge) is "explain".

Commonly used command words in Higher Business Management

Identify is the most straightforward command word, and a short answer is all that is required. For example, "Identify a source of finance for a business".

The answer could be as simple as *"A loan from a bank"*. However, there will be few identify marks available at Higher level so don't count on being able to give many short answers.

Describe requires a more detailed answer, giving the main features. It must be a description of something. Additional marks may be available if you give examples in, or further depth to, your description. These are sometimes referred to as development points.

For example, *"A loan from a bank which is repaid over time in equal instalments with interest"*.

Outline is similar to describe but can be worded in such a way that a more detailed answer is actually required.

For example, *"Outline the impact on a business if banks raise interest rates"*.

To get the mark, you would need to write more than *"They would have to make higher payments on bank loans"*. You would have to add *"which will increase costs to the business, which may lower profits"* to show the impact.

However, if you were to answer a question such as, "Outline the main stages of the recruitment process", the answer required could simply be a list.

Discuss normally requires you to give advantages and disadvantages, or both sides of an argument. It is not always necessary to give both sides of the debate to be awarded full marks, provided that your points are fully developed.

For example, "Discuss the use of bank loans for a business".

Answers could include: *"Allows the business to spread repayments over a longer period of time", "Which will help with cash flow"* and *"The business will have to pay interest on the money borrowed"*.

Distinguish requires you to list the differences between two things. It is important to understand that you only get **one mark** for each distinguishing point.

For example, "Distinguish between a bank loan and a mortgage".

To answer this question you need to say what the differences are: *"A bank loan is normally for a short period such as 5 years, whereas a mortgage is for a much longer period such as 30 years"*. Note that this discussion point would be worth only one mark.

Compare is similar in some ways to distinguish, but also allows you to write what is similar as well as what the differences are.

For example, "Compare a bank loan and a mortgage".

Answers could include the distinguishing point above, but also similarities such as *"Both are repaid with added interest"*.

Explain requires a more detailed answer. Essentially it can be thought of as a description plus an explanation of why something is the way it is.

For example, "Explain the disadvantages of a bank loan for a business".

Your answer would need to be developed, such as, *"Added interest would need to be repaid which would adversely affect the costs to the business"*. Added interest on its own would not gain a mark as it does not actually explain why the bank loan is a disadvantage for the business.

Good luck!

Remember that the rewards for passing Higher Business Management are well worth it! Your pass will help you get the future you want for yourself. In the exam, be confident in your own ability. If you're not sure how to answer a question, trust your instincts and just give it a go anyway.

Keep calm and don't panic! GOOD LUCK!

HIGHER

2014 Specimen Question Paper

National
Qualifications
SPECIMEN ONLY

SQO5/H/01

Business Management

Date — Not applicable

Duration — 2 hours and 15 minutes

Total marks — 70

SECTION 1 — 30 marks

Attempt ALL questions.

SECTION 2 — 40 marks

Attempt ALL questions.

Write your answers clearly in the answer booklet provided. In the answer booklet, you must clearly identify the question number you are attempting.

Use **blue** or **black** ink.

It is recommended that you spend 15 minutes reading over the information provided in **SECTION 1** before responding to the questions.

Before leaving the examination room you must give your answer booklet to the Invigilator; if you do not, you may lose all the marks for this paper.

SECTION 1 — 30 marks

Read ALL the following information and attempt ALL the questions that follow.

The following information has been taken from an Annual Report of J Sainsbury plc and is presented as a report to its shareholders.

J Sainsbury plc

Annual Report to shareholders 2013

The Board is pleased to report on another good year for Sainsbury's. Profits have improved and we are continuing to invest significantly in strengthening the business for the future.

Business review

A winning team

We would like to thank our 157,000 colleagues for their efforts in providing excellent customer service. Our people are the face of Sainsbury's and are central to our success. We continue to invest in their training and development, and in ensuring Sainsbury's is a great place to work. Many of our colleagues have benefited from externally certified training qualifications in our seven food colleges. We are delighted that they share in a record bonus of over £90 million this year.

Sainsbury's Bank

Whilst our core business remains supermarkets, the move into banking with Lloyds Banking Group in 1997 has proved profitable. We have now reached an agreement to acquire Lloyds' 50 per cent shareholding and take full ownership of Sainsbury's Bank.

Our values

Our unique values and strong corporate culture are at the heart of our success and this remains as true today as it was when we were founded 144 years ago. Through our ambitious *20×20 Sustainability Plan* we aim to:

- *Source raw materials with integrity* — by ensuring our products ensure sustainability, eg responsibly caught seafood and no contribution to global deforestation
- *Reduce consumption of unhealthy foods* — by providing clear nutritional information
- *Respect our environment* — by reducing carbon emissions and continuing to use solar energy
- *Be a great place to work* — by providing certificated training for employees
- *Make a positive difference to the community* — by encouraging children to enjoy physical activity

Loyalty and insight

Nearly 12 million Sainsbury's customers regularly use their loyalty card and the data gathered from these cards enables us to understand our customers better and offer them targeted promotions.

Market overview

The UK economic climate in 2012/13 continued to be challenging. Inflation outstripped wage growth, squeezing household budgets. However, consumer confidence is improving due to continued low interest rates and falling unemployment.

Although the outlook has improved slightly over the year, consumer confidence is still lower than it was five years ago due to rising living costs and changes to taxation and benefits. People are buying slightly less in their weekly grocery shop and then topping it up locally in convenience stores.

SECTION 1 (continued)

Customers are more price-conscious than ever, looking for discounts and offers to help them save money. Despite the economic downturn, consumers are still willing to spend money on expensive ethical products such as fair trade items. People carefully consider their spending decisions and have greater expectations of the quality and integrity of goods and services they buy.

Strategy for growth

The following five-point plan highlights our strategy going forward:

- *Great food* — the quality and value of our food, combined with our strong ethical standards and supplier relationships, differentiate us from other supermarkets and help our customers to *Live Well for Less.*

- *Compelling general merchandise and clothing* — *Tu* is the seventh most popular clothing brand in the UK and we sell more bakeware than our rivals.

- *Complementary channels of distribution and services* — we offer a winning mix of supermarkets, convenience stores and an online service.

- *Developing new business* — we continue our drive into the online and digital entertainment market with the purchase of a majority stake in Anobii, now operating as *eBooks by Sainsbury's.* Sainsbury's pharmacies are now open in over 270 stores and in three hospitals. We are finding other new ways to offer our services — from our online retail website to our innovative *Mobile Scan & Go.*

- *Growing space and creating property value* — we are increasing our store portfolio by adding bright, modern extensions, and state-of-the-art new supermarkets and convenience stores.

Source: Adapted from J Sainsbury plc Annual Report 2013

Further information

Exhibit 1 — Extract from Sainsbury's financial performance

	2012/13	2011/12	Change
	£ millions	£ millions	%
Sales	23,303	22,294	+ 4·5
Gross Profit	829	789	+ 5·1
Net Profit	614	598	+ 2.7

Source: Adapted from J Sainsbury plc Annual Report 2013

Exhibit 2 — Sainsbury's market share

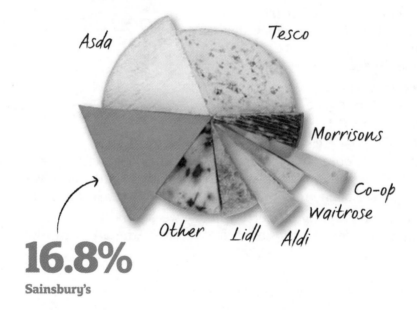

16.8%
Sainsbury's

Source: Kantar Worldpanel total till roll for the 52 weeks to 17 March 2013

Exhibit 3 — Sainsbury's growth timeline

1869	First store opened on London's Drury Lane
1950s	First self-service stores opened
1970s	Introduced the first bakeries, fresh fish counters, coffee shops and petrol stations
1994	First major supermarket in the UK to sell fair trade food
1996	Began recycling partnership with Oxfam
1997	Started Sainsbury's Bank in a joint venture with Lloyds Banking Group
2004	Launched the *Tu* fashion range
2009	First major retailer to stop selling eggs from caged hens
2010	Opened the first of our seven food colleges — with over 20,000 colleagues given off-the-job training
2012	Sainsbury's was the only sponsor for the 2012 Paralympic Games and was a major partner of the Diamond Jubilee celebrations Purchased majority stake in e-book business Anobii

Source: Adapted from J Sainsbury plc Annual Report 2013

MARKS

The following questions are based on ALL the information provided and on knowledge and understanding you have gained whilst studying the Course.

1. (a) (i) Describe what is meant by market share.   1

(ii) Describe People, Process and Physical Evidence used by Sainsbury's in the information provided.   3

(b) Discuss the methods of growth used by Sainsbury's in the information provided.   6

(c) Describe, using evidence from the information provided, ethical and environmental factors Sainsbury's has taken into account.   5

(d) Describe the profitability ratios used to analyse financial data.   3

(e) Explain the impact on Sainsbury's of the external factors highlighted in the information provided.   6

(f) Compare Sainsbury's method of staff training with on-the-job training.   4

(g) Describe the interdependence of Sainsbury's stakeholders identified in the information provided.   2

MARKS

SECTION 2 — 40 marks

Attempt ALL questions

1. (a) Describe the selection methods used to appoint new employees.   4

    (b) Explain the benefits of using information technology to deliver staff training.   3

    (c) Describe one theory of motivation used by managers.   3

2. (a) Describe the reasons a profitable organisation may experience cashflow problems.   4

    (b) Discuss the advantages and disadvantages of using ratio analysis.   6

3. (a) Describe the production methods an organisation could use.   4

    (b) Discuss the use of a just-in-time stock control system.   6

4. (a) Describe the benefits of maintaining a product portfolio.   4

    (b) Compare the use of penetration pricing with skimming pricing.   3

    (c) Describe into the pipeline promotions that an organisation could use.   3

[END OF SPECIMEN QUESTION PAPER]

[BLANK PAGE]

DO NOT WRITE ON THIS PAGE

HIGHER

2015

H

National
Qualifications
2015

X710/76/11

Business Management

MONDAY, 11 MAY

1:00 PM – 3:15 PM

Total marks — 70

SECTION 1 — 30 marks

Attempt ALL questions.

SECTION 2 — 40 marks

Attempt ALL questions.

It is recommended that you spend 15 minutes reading over the information provided in **SECTION 1** before responding to the questions.

Write your answers clearly in the answer booklet provided. In the answer booklet, you must clearly identify the question number you are attempting.

Use **blue** or **black** ink.

Before leaving the examination room you must give your answer booklet to the Invigilator; if you do not, you may lose all the marks for this paper.

SECTION 1 — 30 marks

Read ALL the following information and attempt ALL the questions that follow.

Welcome to the Google plex!

Internet giant to build futuristic headquarters

INTRODUCTION

Google plc, the internet giant, has planned a massive expansion of its Californian headquarters (HQ). The 2·5 million square foot headquarters, commonly referred to as the "Googleplex", is in the midst of an approval process. This is the first time the company has commissioned a building to be designed from scratch rather than modifying premises built by others. Google will have a building designed exactly for its own purpose and one which takes staff needs into account.

CORPORATE SOCIAL RESPONSIBILITY (CSR)

Google's HQ plans to have solar panels and charging stations for employees' electric cars or indeed Google's own "driverless" cars that transport employees around the district. A low-energy heating and cooling system will allow Google to supply 100 percent fresh air economically. Most existing buildings introduce only a small percentage of fresh air. The company also seeks to eliminate potentially harmful chemicals in building materials. Google also have their own charity called "Google.org" and one of their commitments is to encourage the use of renewable energy in the United States of America.

GOOGLE'S PRODUCT PORTFOLIO

The need for a new HQ comes as Google has grown by developing many new products. It has also acquired other technology companies over the years (see Exhibit 1). Products range from the original Google search engine to the Android mobile operating system for smartphones and tablets. Google's product portfolio can be seen in more detail in Exhibit 2.

Twin Design/shutterstock.com

CORPORATE CULTURE

Google has a very relaxed corporate culture and this has been taken into account in the planning of the building. Although employees can work from outwith the office, the new HQ has been designed to encourage employees to want to be there so that they benefit from regular communication and idea sharing. Most Google employees have flexible working hours, adding to the general feeling of wellbeing.

The design will also allow employees to meet up easily and chat. Employees can wear their own casual clothes and pedal on free bicycles or walk to informal meetings in the roof gardens or coffee shops. The Googleplex will continue to use the preferred Google colour scheme of primary colours currently used in the existing HQ and will house impressive facilities. Google's offices are well-known for their perks such as gourmet cafes, sleep pods, laptops attached to gym equipment and even pool tables and bowling alleys!

RECRUITMENT AND SELECTION

Google's new employees are called "Nooglers". It may soon face competition in employing the very best potential "Nooglers" because other technology giants are also improving their offices. These rival businesses wish to ensure that they, like Google, can attract the best talent in the competitive job market.

Google and their competitors recruit for vacancies outwith their current staff from the same pool of University graduates and the wider workforce. Apple, its main competitor, is currently building an even bigger environmentally friendly campus. Meanwhile, Facebook is trying to tempt the next generation of IT graduates by creating a "Main Street" of stores, restaurants and facilities at the centre of its headquarters.

[Turn over

Exhibit 1 — Google's timeline

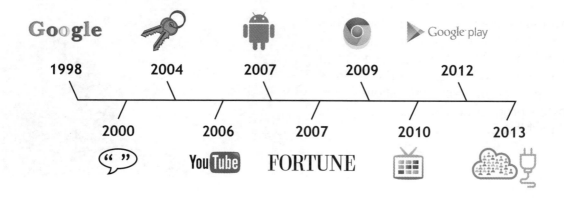

1998 — Google.com
Google.com is registered as a domain.

2000 — Google in 10 Languages
The first 10 languages of Google are released. Today, search is available in 150+ languages.

2004 — Move to new HQ
Google move to their Mountainview headquarters, 11 years before the move to their latest "Googleplex" HQ.

2006 — YouTube acquired
Google announce the takeover of YouTube.

2007 — Android
Google launch Android — the first open platform for smartphone devices.

2007 — "Fortune" Best Company to Work For
Google is rated no 1 company to work for in a well-known business magazine.

2009 — Google Chrome
Google launch their own web browser, Google Chrome.

2010 — Google TV
Google TV is launched.

2012 — Google Play
Android Market is rebranded Google Play, a digital content store offering apps, games, books, music and more.

2013 — Energy efficiency in the cloud
Google funded research shows that increased use of cloud computing would drastically reduce energy consumption.

Exhibit 2 — Google's Product Portfolio

		Market Share	
		High	Low
Market Growth	**High**	• Android mobile operating system • YouTube • Gmail	• Google Chrome internet browser • Google Nexus smartphone • Google TV
	Low	• Google search engine	• Google self-driving cars

Exhibit 3 — Extract from Google's financial statements for the years 2011-2013

Google plc Income Statement (Trading, Profit and Loss Account) 2011-2013

	2011 $ Million		2012 $ Million		2013 $ Million	
Revenue (Sales)		$37,905		$50,175		$59,825
Less Cost of Sales		$13,188		$20,634		$25,858
GROSS PROFIT		**$24,717**		**$29,541**		**$33,967**
Less Expenses						
Sales & Advertising	$4,589		$6,143		$7,253	
Research & Development	$5,162		$6,793		$7,952	
Administration	$3,224		$3,845		$4,796	
		$12,975		$16,781		$20,001
PROFIT FOR THE YEAR (Net Profit)		**$11,742**		**$12,760**		**$13,966**

[Turn over

MARKS

The following questions are based on ALL the information provided and on knowledge and understanding you have gained whilst studying the course.

1. (a)   (i) Describe the method of production used to create Google's new headquarters.

1

   (ii) Discuss the advantages and disadvantages of the method of production described in 1(a)(i).

5

   (b) Describe the advantages to Google of having a varied product portfolio as shown in Exhibit 2.

5

   (c) Explain the benefits of Google's corporate culture to the organisation and its employees.

4

   (d) As a plc, Google has to publish its final accounts as shown in Exhibit 3.

   (i) Describe the following financial terms:

   •   Revenue (Sales);
   •   Gross Profit.

2

   (ii) Describe the trend in profitability using examples from Exhibit 3.

1

   (e) Google's development of its new headquarters is an example of organic (internal) growth.

   Describe other methods of growth available to Google.

4

   (f) Google aims to attract the best available talent from outwith its current staff.

   Discuss the use of this method of recruitment.

5

   (g) Describe the ways in which Google demonstrates positive Corporate Social Responsibility (CSR) as shown in the case study.

3

MARKS

SECTION 2 — 40 marks

Attempt ALL questions

2. (a) Describe the sales promotions which could be used when launching a new product.   4

   (b) Discuss the factors an organisation might consider before selecting a channel of distribution.   4

   (c) Compare the use of random sampling and quota sampling when carrying out market research.   2

3. (a) Discuss the advantages and disadvantages of centralised stock storage.   4

   (b) Explain the disadvantages of just in time stock control.   4

   (c) Describe the benefits of achieving Fairtrade certification.   2

4. (a) Describe the advantages to an organisation of using cash budgets.   4

   (b) Describe the reasons why a competitor may be interested in the financial information of an organisation.   2

   (c) Discuss the sources of long-term finance available to a plc.   4

5. (a) Describe the features of Maslow's motivation theory.   4

   (b) Explain the benefits of positive employee relations.   3

   (c) Discuss the effects of the Equality Act 2010 on an organisation.   3

[END OF QUESTION PAPER]

[BLANK PAGE]

DO NOT WRITE ON THIS PAGE

HIGHER

2016

National
Qualifications
2016

X710/76/11

Business Management

FRIDAY, 27 MAY

9:00 AM — 11:15 AM

Total marks — 70

SECTION 1 — 30 marks

Attempt ALL questions.

SECTION 2 — 40 marks

Attempt ALL questions.

It is recommended that you spend 15 minutes reading over the information provided in **SECTION 1** before responding to the questions.

Write your answers clearly in the answer booklet provided. In the answer booklet, you must clearly identify the question number you are attempting.

Use **blue** or **black** ink.

Before leaving the examination room you must give your answer booklet to the Invigilator; if you do not, you may lose all the marks for this paper.

SECTION 1 — 30 marks

Read ALL the following information and attempt ALL the questions that follow.

Mackie's of Scotland: Greener the better

Luxury ice cream producer Mackie's of Scotland is not shy about promoting its green aspirations. The company states that it wants to become a global brand, and in terms of sustainability, the greenest company in Britain.

Ice cream, crisps and chocolate

Mackie's runs its operations from a 1,600 acre dairy farm in Aberdeenshire where raw materials are sourced from neighbouring farms. The company has a 7% share of the total UK ice cream market with sales of over 10 million litres every year.

In 2004 Mackie's launched "Mackice" by selling ice cubes made from locally sourced spring water. In 2009 Mackie's branched out into crisps when it formed a joint venture with Perthshire-based potato processor Taypack. It now exports to markets in over 20 countries and has expanded into the chocolate confectionery market.

Driven by the desire for absolute customer satisfaction, Mackie's has invested in computer controlled mass-production machinery so that 6,000 litres of ice cream per hour can be produced in order to cope with increasing demand. Products go through rigorous quality assurance and control measures before goods are released for distribution to retailers. There is also a highly trained taste panel which benchmarks new products with competitors.

Investment in renewable energy

One of Mackie's most ambitious goals incorporates the entire site: to become 100% self-sufficient in renewable energy. This fits with the Scottish Government's target of generating the equivalent of 100% of Scotland's gross national electricity consumption from renewable sources by 2020.

Mackie's installed its first 50 kW wind turbine in 1983 which produced enough energy to heat a piggery. The technology applied to wind farms has improved drastically in the intervening years and, via the three modern turbines currently on site, Mackie's has an installed renewable energy capacity of 2·5 MW.

Mackie's estimates that since the installation of the turbines, it has saved approximately 3,480 tonnes of carbon emissions that would otherwise have been produced by the company's day-to-day operations.

Mackie's Marketing Director, Karin Hayhow, said: "The wind turbines are incredibly efficient and have performed much better than expected, largely due to the good location we occupy and the fact that Scotland is the windiest country in Europe".

"However we also have a lot of other exciting projects, such as having on-site injection moulders to make our own tubs." This required an investment of over £1 million and reduced emissions from not having to import packaging from Sweden.

As well as utilising wind to produce energy, Mackie's is also harnessing solar power. In February 2012 150 kW of solar panels were installed on the site. "Through this, we are saving almost £500,000 per year on our electricity bills, and with electricity prices increasing, our savings are only set to rise. This enables us to invest in more efficient machinery and processes that, in turn, help to keep the cost of production down."

Looking to the future

Mackie's is in no way finished with its energy efficiency campaign and has a series of projects that it is looking to implement in the near future:

- Construct a fourth wind turbine.
- Build a 1·5 MW solar farm to increase renewable capacity.
- Invest in electric vehicles on the farm for the use of staff.

Mackie's Finance Director, Gerry Stephens, said: "For any business, managing the bottom line is essential, and cutting energy costs as well as reducing carbon emissions should always be included in any robust business plan."

[Turn over

Further Information

Exhibit 1

Overview of Mackie's renewable and sustainability

Solar Energy	The company has over 700 solar panels which generate electricity to power various parts of the farm and the milking robots.
Zero Waste Water	Waste water is pumped back over the land. The cows also drink the clean waste water.
Natural Fertiliser	The slurry from the cows is used as natural fertiliser, reducing the amount of commercial fertiliser which is bought.
Harnessing Wind	Mackie's commercial turbine was installed in 2005 with a further investment of £1·7 million to add two more in 2007. These two new turbines have more than trebled the electricity generated, saving the company £280,000 a year in electricity bills. Mackie's makes a surplus of energy which is sold to the company Good Energy.
Recycling Packaging	Mackie's recycles cardboard, plastic, wood, batteries and metal.

Adapted from: mackies.co.uk; thescottishfarmer.co.uk

Exhibit 2

Additional information on marketing activities

2002	2004	2010	2012	2013
Official ice cream sponsor of the World Cup in South Korea.	Launched low fat chocolate iced dessert suitable for diabetics.	Sponsor of the Macrobert JustGiving appeal to support deprived families.	New website to promote news, competitions and get valuable customer feedback.	Launched a television advert to further promote its ice cream.

Adapted from: mackies.co.uk

Exhibit 3

Extract from Mackie's social media site informing customers of special offers

Mackie's Ice Cream
12 September

Great offer at Tesco Scottish stores only . . . 1 litre Traditional, Honeycomb, Strawberry, Chocolate, Chocolate Mint and Raspberry Ripple — SAVE £1. Offer ends 15th September. Happy shopping!

Like · Comment · Share   200 Shares

118 people like this

[Turn over

Exhibit 4

Summary of financial performance

	2011 £	2012 £	2013 £
Revenue (Sales)	11,629,244	11,509,252	10,284,432
Gross Profit	5,079,814	4,913,867	4,322,633
Profit for year (Net Profit)	255,682	197,079	546,801

Adapted from: companieshouse.gov.uk

MARKS

The following questions are based on ALL the information provided and on knowledge and understanding you have gained whilst studying the course.

1. (a) (i) Describe **2** suitable pricing strategies for Mackie's luxury ice cream produce.

   4

   (ii) Discuss the "out of the pipeline" methods of promotion identified in the case study.

   4

   (b) Explain, using examples from the case study, the benefits to Mackie's of having a diverse product portfolio.

   4

   (c) Describe the reasons why Mackie's heavily invested in renewable energy methods.

   3

   (d) Compare the method of production used by Mackie's with job production.

   4

   (e) Discuss the methods of ensuring quality identified in the case study.

   5

   (f) (i) Describe the ratios which could be calculated from the financial information in **Exhibit 4**.

   3

   (ii) Using **Exhibit 4**, explain the trends in Mackie's profits.

   3

[Turn over for next question

MARKS

SECTION 2 — 40 marks
Attempt ALL questions

2. (a) Describe the methods which may be used to motivate employees.   4

    (b) Explain the benefits of an appraisal system.   4

    (c) Describe the benefits of workforce planning.   2

3. (a) Explain the advantages of internal (organic) growth.   4

    (b) Discuss the use of geographical grouping.   3

    (c) Describe the advantages of being a social enterprise.   3

4. (a) (i) Describe the impact of competition policy on an organisation.   2

        (ii) Other than competition, explain the impact of external factors on an organisation.   5

    (b) Distinguish between a tactical decision and an operational decision.   3

5. (a) Justify the use of spreadsheets within the finance department.   4

    (b) Other than spreadsheets, describe how modern technology can be used by the finance department.   6

[END OF QUESTION PAPER]

HIGHER

2017

H

National Qualifications 2017

X710/76/11

Business Management

TUESDAY, 16 MAY

9:00 AM — 11:15 AM

Total marks — 70

SECTION 1 — 30 marks

Attempt ALL questions

SECTION 2 — 40 marks

Attempt ALL questions

It is recommended that you spend 15 minutes reading over the information provided in **SECTION 1** before responding to the questions.

Write your answers clearly in the answer booklet provided. In the answer booklet, you must clearly identify the question number you are attempting.

Use **blue** or **black** ink.

Before leaving the examination room you must give your answer booklet to the Invigilator; if you do not, you may lose all the marks for this paper.

Section 1 of this Question Paper replaces the original SQA Past Paper 2017, which cannot be reproduced for copyright reasons. As such, it should be stressed that it is not an official SQA-verified section, although every care has been taken by the Publishers to ensure that it offers appropriate practice material for Higher Business Management.

SECTION 1 — 30 marks

Read ALL the following information and attempt ALL the questions that follow.

The following information has been taken from the Mary's Meals website.

Mary's Meals

Mary's Meals is a charity that works to support a school feeding programme for over 920,000 children across the world. It all started in 1992 when two brothers, Magnus and Fergus MacFarlane-Barrow, were watching the television news coverage of the Bosnian conflict. They started an appeal for food and blankets and filled a Jeep and drove to Bosnia. When they returned and went back to work, they discovered that donations were still arriving. Magnus gave up his job for a year and kept making trips to Bosnia with donations. The donations didn't stop and Magnus set up a charity, Scottish International Relief, which expanded its work into Romania, Liberia and Croatia. By 2002, the charity was supporting a famine relief project in Malawi. As Magnus helped support the children of a mother who was dying of AIDS, the inspiration for Mary's Meals was born: to provide chronically hungry children with one meal every school day. This helps to encourage children to gain education and lift them out of poverty. By 2014, the charity now known as Mary's Meals was providing meals to children in Africa, Asia, the Caribbean, Eastern Europe and South America.

A simple solution to world hunger

For many children, Mary's Meals may be the only meal they will have in a day. In Malawi, it costs £8.20 to provide Mary's Meals to one child for a whole school year and an average of £12.20 per child per year globally. The meals are made using locally produced food wherever possible. This respects local culture and tastes and avoids transport costs.

The charity also works in partnership with local communities wherever possible. In Malawi, over 60,000 volunteers cook and serve over 600,000 meals every school day.

Mary's Meals aims to spend at least 93p of every £1 that is donated to carry out charitable work. It does this by making extensive use of volunteers and by monitoring and controlling costs to keep them as low as possible.

It works with other partner organisations and supports other charitable work. (See Exhibit 1 and Exhibit 3 for more information.)

Ethical and morally responsible business practice

Mary's Meals can be seen to be an ethical business model. It exists to provide a service to people using resources that have been donated by other people. The Mary's Meals vision is that every child receives one daily meal in their place of education, and that all those who have more than they need share with those who lack even the most basic things.

The mission of the charity is to enable people to offer their money, goods, skills, time, or prayer, and through this involvement, providing the most effective help to those suffering the effects of extreme poverty in the world's poorest communities.

Donations

Mary's Meals is dependent on donations of money in order to operate. The Mary's Meals website is available in different languages and you can make a donation online. It is also possible to make a regular donation to the charity from your bank account or donate by phone, by text or by post. Some people may choose to keep a donation box in their home and encourage visitors who come for dinner to make a donation to Mary's Meals.

Counting on support from around the globe, Mary's Meals has fundraising entities and registered charity arms in Austria, Canada, Croatia, France, Germany, Italy, Ireland, the Netherlands, Portugal, Spain, the United Kingdom and the USA. It promotes the fact that a maximum of 7p in every £1 donated is used for corporate governance.

Source: http://www.marysmeals.org.uk

[Turn over

Further Information

Exhibit 1 — Mary's Meals projects and partnership working

Use of celebrities	Celebrities help raise the profile of the work of the charity, eg Hollywood star Gerard Butler recently visited Mary's Meals in Liberia
The backpack project	Over 420,000 donated backpacks have been sent overseas to help children attending school
Saving Grace	A short animation telling the story of 10-year-old Grace
Sponsor a school	Rather than making a donation to the charity, people or groups are encouraged to sponsor an entire school
Stage a screening of Child 31	A film made to raise awareness of the work of Mary's Meals

Exhibit 2 — Key statistics

Mary's Meals Charity

		Unrestricted funds £	Restricted funds £	2013 Total £	2012 Total £
Incoming resources					
Incoming resources from generated funds:					
Voluntary income	2	8,043,912	3,837,541	11,881,453	7,755,910
Activities for generating funds	3	559,809	—	559,809	1,893,901
Investment income		11,801	—	11,801	8,839
Incoming resources from charitable activities		917	—	917	360
Tax reclaimed on Gift Aid		452,315	16,000	468,315	334,666
Total incoming resources		9,068,754	3,853,541	12,922,295	9,993,676

Exhibit 3 — Facts at a glance

- Total number of children receiving a daily meal in school = 894,288
- Average global cost of Mary's Meals per child, per year = £12.20
- Worldwide average cost per meal = 6 pence
- Number of chronically hungry children in the world = 300 million (around 57 million of these children are out of school)
- Number of backpacks sent overseas in 2014 (so far) = 20,872
- Total number of backpacks delivered to date = 402,680
- In addition to school feeding projects, Mary's Meals supports a children's home project in Romania

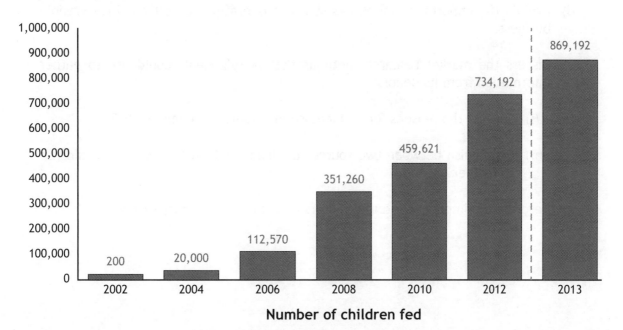

Number of children fed

Exhibit 4 — How money is spent

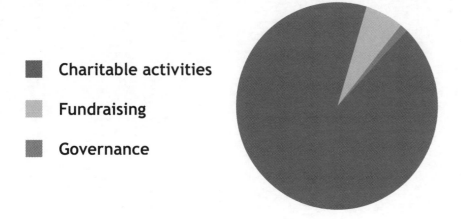

■ **Charitable activities**

■ **Fundraising**

■ **Governance**

[Turn over

MARKS

The following questions are based on ALL the information provided and on knowledge and understanding whilst studying the course.

1. (a) Using the case study, compare the objectives of Mary's Meals to a public sector organisation.   **3**

    (b) Discuss the potential areas of conflict for Mary's Meals as it mostly operates in overseas countries.   **5**

    (c) Describe the promotional strategies used by Mary's Meals to attract donations.   **5**

    (d) Explain the importance for Mary's Meals to operate as an ethically responsible business.   **3**

    (e) Discuss the market research methods that Mary's Meals could use to gather information from its donors.   **6**

    (f)   (i) Suggest the reasons for an increase in voluntary income in 2013.   **2**

         (ii) Distinguish between two sources of finance which Mary's Meals could use to further expand.   **2**

    (g) Describe the impact of internal factors on a charity like Mary's Meals.   **4**

MARKS

SECTION 2 — 40 marks

Attempt ALL questions

2. (a) Explain the benefits to an organisation of developing a strong corporate culture. 3

   (b) Describe the effects of widening the span of control of a manager. 5

   (c) Describe examples of conflict that may arise between different groups of stakeholders. 2

3. (a) Discuss the use of benchmarking to ensure quality. 4

   (b) Describe ways an organisation can become environmentally responsible. 3

   (c) Justify the use of job production. 3

4. (a) Explain the benefits of preparing a cash budget. 5

   (b) Describe the impact on an organisation of having poor cash flow. 5

5. (a) Describe the laissez-faire style of leadership. 3

   (b) Describe the impact of current employment legislation on organisations. 4

   (c) Discuss the costs and benefits of work-based qualifications. 3

[END OF QUESTION PAPER]

[BLANK PAGE]

DO NOT WRITE ON THIS PAGE

Answers

HIGHER BUSINESS MANAGEMENT
2014 SPECIMEN QUESTION PAPER

SECTION 1

Question			Expected answer(s)	Max mark
1	a	i	Responses could include the following: • Market share is an organisation's percentage of the overall sales in a particular market. Accept any other suitable response.	1
		ii	Responses could include the following: **People:** anyone who comes into contact with your customers that will have an effect on customer satisfaction. • Sainsbury's ensures employees are highly trained. • Sainsbury's employees are noted for providing excellent customer service. **Process:** the ways of delivering the service, ie helpfulness of staff, quality of information given. • Providing innovative mobile scan-and-go facilities in stores. • Using e-commerce for purchases. • Using loyalty cards to maintain customer satisfaction. • Offering customers targeted promotions. • Providing nutritional information on food products. **Physical Evidence:** the tangible aspect of delivering the service, ie the building. • Providing bright and modern extensions. • Providing updated state-of-the-art stores. Accept any other suitable response.	3
1	b		Responses could include the following: Organic/internal growth • Growth of a business from its own internally generated resources (1 mark for definition). • Sainsbury's is growing by increasing the number of its state-of-the-art new supermarkets (1 mark for definition). *Advantages* • Less risky than taking over other businesses. • Can be financed through internal funds, eg retained profits. • Builds on a business's strengths, eg brands, customers. *Disadvantages* • Growth may be dependent on the growth of the overall market. • Slower method of growth — shareholders may prefer a more rapid growth. Diversification/takeover • Sainsbury's buying a majority stake in Anobii e-books (1 mark for definition). • Sainsbury's joining with Lloyds Banking Group to form Sainsbury's Bank (1 mark for definition). *Advantages (can apply to diversification or takeover)* • Reduces the risk of business failure. • Makes a larger and more financially secure business. *Disadvantages (can apply to diversification or takeover)* • Requires allocation of significant financial and human resources. • Risk of harming the main company business. Accept any other suitable response within each of the above headings.	6

Question			Expected answer(s)	Max mark
1	c		Responses could include the following: • Suppliers' products ensure sustainability of raw materials. • Sainsbury's commitment to reducing unhealthy food and providing nutritional information. • Suppliers' products don't have a large carbon footprint (1 mark) and support renewable energies (1 development mark). • Sainsbury's commitment to making a positive difference to the communities in which it operates. • Suppliers' products are fair trade (1 mark) meaning suppliers get a fair price for products and are likely to stay in business (1 development mark). • Sainsbury's recycling partnership with Oxfam. • Suppliers ensure high standards of animal welfare. Accept any other suitable response.	5
	d		Responses could include the following: Gross profit ratio • Measures the percentage of profit that is made from buying and selling stock. Net profit ratio • Measures the percentage of profit that is made after expenses are deducted from GP. Return on capital employed • Measures the percentage of investment that is yielded as profit. Accept any other suitable response.	3
	e		Responses could include the following: • *Rising inflation* means goods/services cost more, so Sainsbury's plans to offer more great food of quality and value. • *Low interest rates* mean consumers are less likely to save and so spend more in shops like Sainsbury's (1 mark). For example, Sainsbury's sales have increased by 4·5% (1 mark for development for using Source A). • *Falling unemployment* means consumers may have more wages/disposable income to spend in shops like Sainsbury's. • *Rising living costs,* however, mean that consumers may have less disposable income to spend in Sainsbury's. • *Customers are being more price conscious* so Sainsbury's is offering more promotional offers/deals. • *Consumers are making fewer but more considered spending choices* so are buying higher quality goods such as fair trade products provided by Sainsbury's. • *Competitive factors* — Sainsbury's must be constantly aware of these, eg from Asda and Tesco, to maintain or increase its current market share of 16·8% (Exhibit 2). Accept any other suitable response.	6
	f		Responses could include the following: • Sainsbury's uses off-the-job training which takes place at training colleges away from the workplace, whereas on-the-job training takes place in the workplace. • Sainsbury's uses its own training colleges (off-the-job) which can offer intense training away from the distractions at work, whereas on-the-job training can be distracting. • When at a training college/off-the-job, the employee isn't contributing to the business, whereas with on-the-job training the employee may be doing some work. • With off-the-job training an employee learns from professional trainers/instructors/teachers, whereas with on-the-job training the employee learns from colleagues through demonstrating/coaching. • With off-the-job training the employee is away from colleagues and will still have to integrate when completed, whereas with on-the-job training, employee bonds can be built during the training process. • Sending a new employee to a training college may help them feel better prepared for the job; however, with on-the-job training the employee may feel apprehensive. • Off-the-job training is more expensive than on-the-job training. Accept any other suitable response.	4

Question			Expected answer(s)	Max mark
1	g		Responses could include the following: • Sainsbury's (owners) need employees to operate stores and employees require Sainsbury's to provide secure jobs. • Suppliers need Sainsbury's to buy their stock and Sainsbury's needs suppliers to provide good-quality products. • Employees need customers to give money to Sainsbury's in order to have job security and customers need good-quality service from employees. • Employees need owners for wages/training/career development and owners need employees for productivity/good customer service. • Owners need customers to give them profits/market share and customers need owners for quality services/products. Accept any other suitable response.	2

SECTION 2

Question			Expected answer(s)	Max mark
1	a		Responses could include the following: Application forms • Forms are created to request relevant information from applicants. • Comparison of applicants is easier as all provide the same information. CVs • A written summary of an applicant's experience, educational background and any other relevant information. • Candidates are free to provide the information they feel is relevant, which may not be requested on an application form. Interviews • A formal face-to-face meeting between an employer and an applicant. • Candidates can be compared in a pressure situation. • Allows candidates to respond to questions; they can also ask questions about the job/company. • Interviewers can compare notes to get a consensus on the best applicants. Assessment centres • Candidates can be observed in practical situations. • Tasks can be tailored to the vacancy, eg in-tray exercise, group task, presentation, case study. • Candidates can be moved around to work with a variety of others to see how they perform with different people and personality types. Testing • Attainment testing allows a candidate to demonstrate their skills, eg ICT, joinery skills, childcare skills. • Medical testing measures physical fitness which may be required for certain jobs, eg fire service, armed services, professional football. Accept any other suitable response.	4
	b		Responses could include the following: • Visuals from presentation software provide reinforcement to verbal information from trainer/speaker (1 mark), therefore it holds the attention of the trainees longer (1 development mark). • Staff in remote locations can be involved in training events using web conferencing, reducing the need to travel. • Live-link meetings/online tutorials can be set up between trainer and trainee so support is immediately available. • Staff being trained can access centrally-stored shared files from any geographical location. Accept any other suitable response.	3

Question			Expected answer(s)	Max mark
1	c		Responses could include the following:	3
			<u>Maslow's Hierarchy of Needs</u>	
			• Maslow suggested that there were five interdependent levels of basic human needs (motivators) that must be satisfied in a strict sequence (1 mark), starting with the lowest level and working up to the highest (1 development mark).	
			• Physiological needs (to stay alive and reproduce), and security needs (to feel safe) are the most fundamental and pressing needs (1 mark).	
			• They are followed by social needs (for love and belonging), self-esteem needs (to feel worthy/respected) and, lastly, self-actualisation needs (to realise potential and have status) (1 mark).	
			• You cannot progress to the next level in the hierarchy until the previous level is satisfied (1 mark).	
			<u>McGregor's Theory X and Theory Y</u>	
			• McGregor believed there were two distinct sets of assumptions that managers, in general, have about their employees (1 mark).	
			Theory-X assumptions are:	
			• Most employees dislike work and will avoid it at all costs (1 mark), therefore workers must be continually coerced, controlled and threatened to get the work done (1 development mark).	
			• Employees have little or no ambition/prefer to avoid responsibility and choose security above everything else (1 mark).	
			Theory-Y assumptions are:	
			• Most employees find work to be a source of satisfaction/are generally self-motivated in meeting individual and company goals (1 mark).	
			• Workers either seek responsibility or learn to accept it willingly (1 mark) and are motivated by the needs at the top end of Maslow's hierarchy (1 development mark).	
			<u>Herzberg</u>	
			• Herzberg believed that employee satisfaction is related to factors which motivate, and factors which cause dissatisfaction — hygiene factors (1 mark).	
			• Motivating factors give job satisfaction and include giving employees increased responsibility/recognition for their effort/personal sense of achievement/changes for promotion, etc.	
			• Motivating factors refer to things involved in doing the job.	
			• Hygiene factors need to be met to prevent dissatisfaction and include pay and conditions/support for colleagues/company policies and procedures, etc.	
			• Hygiene factors are things which define the job.	
			Accept any other suitable response.	
2	a		Responses could include the following:	4
			• Too much money tied up in unsold stock.	
			• Customers being given too long a credit period.	
			• Customers being given too high a credit limit.	
			• Owners taking excessive cash drawings.	
			• Suppliers not allowing a trade credit period.	
			• Sudden increase in an expense, eg heat and light.	
			• High capital expenditure outlay in one month instead of spreading payments over a period of time.	
			Accept any other suitable response.	
	b		Responses could include the following:	6
			Advantages	
			• Good for comparing current performance with that of previous years.	
			• Good for comparing with rival businesses.	
			• Highlights differences in performance that will aid future decision-making/financial planning.	
			• Good for highlighting trends over a period of time.	
			Disadvantages	
			• Ratios are based on historic financial information which limits usefulness.	
			• Comparisons only useful if made with like-for-like organisations — firms in the same industry may differ in size/product mix/objectives.	
			• The accounting information used to calculate ratios does not take account of other internal factors, eg quality of managers/staff, staff motivation, staff turnover, location of business.	
			• Calculations do not show the implications of product developments or declining products.	
			• The accounting information used to calculate ratios does not include external factors — PESTEC.	
			Accept any other suitable response.	

Question			Expected answer(s)	Max mark
3	a		Responses could include the following: • Job production – one-off single product is made to a customer's specification (1 mark). This method of production requires highly skilled workers (1 development mark) and the business can charge a premium price for the product (1 development mark). • Batch production – groups of similar products are made at the same time and no item in the batch goes to the next stage until the whole batch is ready. • Flow production – items move continuously from one operation to the next and each part of the process leads to the completion of the final product. • Labour-intensive – production is carried out by a high level of labour. • Capital-intensive – production is carried out using mainly machinery, highly automated production. Accept any other suitable response.	4
	b		Responses could include the following: • Just-in-time (JIT) stock control system reduces storage costs as stock is delivered as it is needed (1 mark). • This means that the organisation is more responsive to consumer demand (1 development mark) and that money is not tied up unnecessarily in buying large volumes of stock (1 development mark). • This can also result in less wastage of stock as it is only being ordered when it is needed (1 development mark). • However, it also means that organisations can lose out on bulk-buying discounts (1 mark). • Having a JIT system relies heavily on suppliers' co-operation in delivering stock when it is needed (1 mark). • Using a JIT system could result in high admin and delivery costs as there are many small deliveries (1 mark). • This could mean that production may be interrupted/halted if there is a delay with a delivery (1 development mark). • Deliveries of small quantities and not holding stock could mean the organisation is unable to meet sudden increases in demand (1 development mark). Accept any other suitable response.	6
4	a		Responses could include the following: • Allows organisation to spread risk (1 mark). If one product's sales decline, another product's sales could be growing (1 development mark). • The opportunity for increased sales/profits from selling different products (1 mark) due to customers having a number of products to buy from one brand (1 development mark). • Seasonal fluctuations can be evened out (1 mark) – the company may not struggle as much if they have products that are popular at certain times of year (1 development mark). • They can meet the needs of different market segments. • Newer products at growth stage can replace those at the decline stage of the product life cycle. • Reference to analysis of Boston Matrix – resources can be allocated from poorer performing products ("dogs") to income-generating products ("stars" or "cash cows"). Accept any other suitable response.	4
	b		Responses could include the following: • Penetration pricing is used in a highly competitive market, whereas skimming pricing is used in a market with little or no competition. • Penetration pricing means that the product will be introduced at a low price, whereas skimming pricing means that the product is introduced at a high price. • With penetration pricing the price will be increased once the product has been established, whereas with skimming pricing the price is decreased as competition enters the market. • Penetration pricing is used to entice consumers to switch from other brands, whereas skimming pricing is used when the product is new or unique. • Both penetration and skimming pricing are short-term pricing strategies. • Both penetration and skimming pricing are used when introducing new products to the market. Accept any other suitable response.	3

Question			Expected answer(s)	Max mark
4	c		Responses could include the following: • These are promotions that a manufacturer gives to the wholesaler or retailer that sells their products (definition). • Dealer loaders are one example of 'into the pipeline promotion': this involves the wholesaler/retailer receiving an extra amount free, eg five boxes for the price of four. • The manufacturer may also provide the wholesaler/retailer with staff training. • The manufacturer may provide the wholesaler/retailer with point of-sale displays. • The manufacturer could allow sale-or-return. Accept any other suitable response.	3

HIGHER BUSINESS MANAGEMENT
2015

SECTION 1

Question			Expected answer(s)	Max mark
1	a	i	• The type of production used to produce Google's headquarters is Job Production which is producing a single product/one off product/products to exact requirements	1
		ii	**Advantages** • The headquarters can be designed to exact specifications • A higher price can be charged • It allows the customer to change the design/make alterations during the process • More motivated staff • Will improve an organisation's competitiveness if it is the only one that can provide non-standard products **Disadvantages** • The wages paid will need to be higher to reflect staff skills • This will increase the overall final price of the product which may put some customers off • There can be higher than average R&D costs • Costs are high as a variety of machinery/tools are required which may often be laying idle • Lead times can be lengthy	5
	b		• Allows organisation to spread risk over different markets • Can meet the needs of different market segments • 'Cash cows' can fund other, riskier, ventures • 'Stars' can allow a business to be a market leader • 'Problem Child' products give businesses opportunity to invest • 'Dogs' should be divested • Increased profits can arise from selling different products • Newer products can replace those at the end of the life cycle • A range of products increases brand awareness • Easier to launch new products with large existing portfolio	5

	c		• Google uses flexible working patterns which means staff work when is best suited to them/when they are most productive
			• Staff can work from home/where they want which might motivate them to be more productive
			• Open plan/relaxed office layout encourages collaboration which means better communication and idea sharing
			  • This will also lead to better decisions being made
			• Perks such as pool tables, bowling alleys, gyms etc will mean staff are motivated and will work to a better standard
			  • This will also mean staff turnover will also be low meaning quality trained staff aren't lost to competition
			  • Perks will also attract the best staff to Google meaning they have an advantage over the competition
			• Roof gardens, coffee shops etc will encourage staff to communicate with each other in a relaxed informal way, leading to better decision making
			• Casual dress code will mean there is a relaxed environment in which to work in/will mean staff want to come to the office
			• Strong corporate identity through corporate colours/language and jargon etc which will mean employees feel part of the organisation
			• Use of relaxed and informal language means staff feel comfortable working there and perform well
				4

	d	i	• Revenue (sales): The amount of money received for selling goods or services during the year • Gross Profit: The profit made from buying and selling OR • GP is calculated by deducting cost of sales from sales revenue	2
		ii	Possible trends include: • Profit has increased • Gross profit has increased • Profit for the year (Net Profit) has increased	1

Question		Expected answer(s)	Max mark
e		**Horizontal integration** • Google could acquire (takeover) or merge with a business in the same sector of industry as it **Vertical integration** • Google could acquire (takeover) or merge with a business in an earlier (backward) or • Later (forward) sector of industry as it **Conglomerate integration/diversification** • Google could acquire (takeover) or merge with a business in a completely different market **Outsourcing** • Google could contract out some of its procedures (eg catering, admin etc) • To allow it to concentrate on core activities **Divestment** • Google could sell off parts of its business to raise money to fund external growth eg takeover Management buy-in… Merger… Takeover… Asset stripping…	4

f		**Advantages**
		• Fresh, new ideas/skills are brought into the business
		• Wider pool of talent to choose from
		• There is no 'gap' created by promoting from within
		• It can avoid jealousy being created from one existing staff member being promoted over another
		Disadvantages
		• Timely to recruit and select from such a vast pool
		• Induction training will have to be carried out
		  • Production time lost
		  • Can be costly
		• Staff may be de-motivated because there is no internal promotion
		• New employee is unknown to the organisation
			5

g		• Google has a charitable arm called Google.org which promotes renewable energy
		• Funding environmental research proves Google is willing to pay to help the environment
		• Google uses solar panels at the Googleplex to reduce its carbon footprint
		• Google focuses on air quality/letting less harmful chemicals into the environment
		• Google offers free EV charging stations for employees' vehicles to reduce emissions
		• Google treats its staff well eg
		  • Publicity in Fortune: Best Company To Work For
		  • Perks such as flexible working, gym equipment etc
			3

SECTION 2

Question			Expected answer(s)	Max mark
2	a		• Free samples to try • Free entry to competitions • Demonstrations of products — let customers see/try new product before buying • Credit facilities allow customers to buy and pay back over a period of time • Free gift with purchase of the new product • BOGOF — buy new product, get another item free • Free delivery with purchase • Offering discounts/promotional pricing	4
	b		• Type of Product — suitable transportation/storage for type of product; product durability eg electrical, frozen food, flowers, liquid, livestock • Finance available — if finance is limited this may affect the choice of channel selected • Image of Product — channel should reflect the quality of the product eg high quality distributed through exclusive, up-market retailers • Legal restrictions — some products can only be sold in certain ways/places eg cigarettes/alcohol/medicines • Where the product is in its life cycle — as it progresses through growth to maturity it needs to be more available to the market • Distribution capability of the organisation — does it have transport or does this need to be outsourced • Technical products — if highly technical it may need to be demonstrated through direct sales	4

Question			Expected answer(s)	Max mark
	c		• Random sampling is when respondents are picked randomly **whereas** quota is picked from a group of people with specific characteristics • Random uses pre-selected respondents who must be interviewed **whereas** quota allows researcher to find respondents who fit the characteristics required • Random is expensive to carry out because specific respondents must be interviewed and contacted until they are available **whereas** quota is less expensive as the interviewer simply needs to find suitable respondents • Random sampling reduces biased results because of method of selection of respondents but bias can occur with quota sampling as the interviewer decides who to question Accept any other suitable response.	2
3	a		**Advantages** • Stock may be ordered in bulk and economies of scale taken advantage of • Reduced risk of pilferage as staff may be employed to monitor issues of stock • Stock is maintained in appropriate conditions which reduces waste • No space is taken up in departments with storage • Specialist staff handle stock more efficiently • Centralised warehouse can be cheaper than using multiple warehouses • Centralised ensures consistent stock handling procedures **Disadvantages** • More time is taken to access stock — physically moving the stock to department and the paperwork involved • Additional staff increases costs • Cost of specialist equipment and storage facilities • Not reflective of actual stock usage in each division/branch	4

	b		• It is harder to cope with unexpected changes in demand which means customers may go elsewhere
			• If customers are forced to go elsewhere for a product they may be lost completely to a competitor
			• Could cause delays in production or possibly halt production as there are no raw materials to use in production
			  • Which can mean paying for workers who aren't producing any goods
			• Continually ordering stock can mean increased administration costs
			• Increased transport costs due to the number of deliveries taking place
			  • Can also increase carbon footprint
			• Increased unit costs due to making small orders as opposed to buying in bulk
			• Relies on good communication/relationships with suppliers to work effectively
				4

	c		• Fairtrade certification improves the image of the organisation • Attracts consumers who have positive attitudes towards products which are ethically made • The Fairtrade trademark can be used as a marketing tool • The trademark shows international standards have been met • Higher prices can be charged for Fairtrade products • May attract staff who wish to work for an ethical company	2
4	a		• They help to highlight periods when cash flow problems may occur; • This allows the organisation to take corrective action • Cash budgets can be used to secure borrowing/show potential investors • They can be used to make comparisons between actual spending and targeted spending • They can show periods of surplus cash which could be used for capital investment • They can be used to give departments/managers a budget/target to focus on • They can be used to aid future financial planning • They can help to measure performance of organisation/departments Accept any other suitable response.	4
	b		• To measure the organisation's market share • To compare costs eg expenses • To compare GP%/NP% • To find out if they may be a target for takeover • To help their own decision making • To compare prices • To offer better salaries Accept any other suitable response.	2

Question			Expected answer(s)	Max mark
	c		**Share issue** • Shareholders become owners of plc which may mean founders lose control • Large sums of money can be raised by this method **Government grant** • May take a long time to secure the grant • Must meet specific conditions to secure grant • Does not have to be paid back **Bank loan** • Simple and fast way to increase finance in business • Interest charges may affect cash flow in a negative way • Repaid in instalments which aids budgeting **Commercial mortgage** • Repaid with interest over long term **Debentures** • Interest is charged and may affect cash flow **Venture capital/business angels** • Will provide capital when banks think it is too risky; advise and support may also be provided to help improve/grow the business **Hire purchase...** **Leasing...**	4
5	a		• Maslow's theory classifies human needs and how they are related to each other (hierarchy) • A person starts at the bottom of the hierarchy and will initially seek to satisfy basic needs eg food and shelter • These can be satisfied through pay • Once these needs have been satisfied they are no longer a motivator • The next level which is security and protection (safety needs) • Job security/safe working environment • The next level is social/love and belonging needs where most people want to belong to a group • Working with colleagues who provide support, teamwork communication • Esteem needs are about being given recognition for a job well done • A promotion might achieve this • Self-actualisation is how people realise their potential • May be measured by the extent of success and/or challenge at work • If management can identify which level each employee has reached they can decide on suitable rewards	4
	b		• Employees will have their chance to discuss changes or grievances so will feel happier and more secure in the workplace • It will be easier to introduce change within the organisation as staff will become flexible with suggestions from management • Disputes are less likely to arise as the workers will have been consulted and understand what it is that the employer is trying to achieve through the changes and why the changes are necessary • Good employee relations mean that the workforce will be committed and will help ensure the business meets its objectives • The organisation will gain a good image for treating its employees correctly and maintaining good employee relations and therefore will attract new employees easily	3
	c		• Avoids discrimination within the workplace • Requires organisations to promote equality • They must ensure that their recruitment policies are compliant with the act • They must have comprehensive anti-discrimination and harassment policies in place • Action needs to be taken against barriers that prevent employees with protected characteristics from carrying out their job, making it accessible for them • Ensuring disability access in the workplace may be costly • The organisation must investigate any accusations of discrimination and take action where necessary • The organisation may face legal action • Could result in fines/sanctions • Reputation may be negatively affected	3

HIGHER BUSINESS MANAGEMENT
2016

SECTION 1

Question			Expected answer(s)	Max mark
1	a	i	**Premium pricing** • A high price is set • Can give an impression of quality/exclusive image **Competitive pricing** • Price is set similar to competitors • Requires effective promotion/advertising **Market skimming** • Price is initially set high but will lower over time • Customers may want to try the product when it is introduced • High profit margins during the introduction stage help recover costs • Over time the price decreases • Effective for new product launches with few competitors **Penetration pricing** • May be used to launch ice cream into a new market • A low price is initially set • With more sales over time the price will increase **Promotional pricing** • Vouchers/offers/discounts are used to encourage customers to buy • Price may be lowered for a period of time • Used to quickly sell stock and aid cash flow Loss leader... Destroyer pricing... Psychological pricing... Cost-plus pricing...	4
		ii	**Special offers/Save £1/Discount** • Price can be lowered for a period of time • Useful promotion method for shifting stock • Encourages new customers to purchase • Retain loyal customers • Can lower potential profit margin • Customers feel they are getting value for money **Competitions** • Customers have a chance of winning through purchasing a product • May incur additional marketing costs • Can gather marking details from customers, e.g. email, phone number, etc. • Encourages repeat custom to increase the chance of winning	4
	b		• Having different products such as crisps and ice cream spreads the risk therefore reducing the chances of making a loss • Cope with seasonal changes, e.g. ice cream sells well in the summer so can provide higher revenue for this period • All products can be branded, e.g. the crisps and the ice cream produce and therefore enhances the company image • Customers who are loyal may buy multiple products, such as ice cream and chocolate, which will increase sales • Can give a competitive edge to a company encouraging sales over rivals, e.g. selling ice cream suitable for diabetics • The company may be worth more if it were to be sold or parts divested, i.e. selling off crisp production • Can be efficient, e.g. using the same production/employees to make ice cream and ice cubes • Allows for faster growth/easier to expand, e.g. exporting crisps into other countries • Joint venture with Taypack means new skills can be brought in when developing products, e.g. Taypack were potato specialists	4

Question		Expected answer(s)	Max mark

c		• Provides possibly endless energy
		• Reduces running costs by saving the company £500,000/£280,000 a year
		  • Finance saved can be invested into better machinery
		• Scotland is very windy so there is plenty supply for wind turbine energy
		• Surplus of energy is sold for additional income
		• Helps meet the company's objective — to be the greenest company in Britain
		  • Helps meet the Government objective
		  • Can give the company a good image/reputation
		• Reduces emissions — saved 3,480 tonnes of carbon emissions
		• Customers may be attracted to purchase Mackie's goods as they care about the environment
		  • Provide a competitive edge
			3

d		• Job production is labour intensive whereas Mackie's production is more capital intensive • Job production is when one product is made at a time whereas flow/batch/mass production is when multiple products are made at a time • Higher prices may be charged for job production as it is a one-off whereas Mackie's production can spread cost over multiple units/can benefit from economies of scale • Job production can customise individual products but Mackie's production can only customise each batch/run • Job production can be more motivating as the product changes/less repetitive... • Both methods of production can be expensive in terms of staff training and machinery	4
e		**Quality inputs** • Products are carefully sourced from local/reliable suppliers which results in better quality output, e.g. fresher produce (materials) • Staff are trained meaning they are skilled so less likely to make mistakes (labour) • Can be motivating for staff to receive training **Taste panel/Quality circle** • A group of employees who taste the goods to check the quality • May reduce complaints from customers/retailers if produce is checked thoroughly • May empower employees who are involved, increasing motivation **Quality assurance** • Quality checked throughout production • Mistakes are identified quickly reduces waste/saves money • Can be expensive due to the requirement of regular checks **Quality control** • Checks of only inputs and outputs • Cheaper than quality assurance as fewer checks are required **Continuous improvement** • Better machinery can result in better output • Requires a commitment from management **Benchmarking** • Best practice is identified from a competitor/market leader and targets are set • Increases competitiveness • Can be difficult to find a suitable company to benchmark	5
f	i	**Gross Profit ratio** • Gross Profit/Sales Revenue × 100 **OR** Amount of gross profit made from every £ of sales • Percentage of profit made on sales before expenses are deducted/from buying and selling inventory **Profit For The Year ratio** • Profit For The Year/Sales Revenue × 100 **OR** Amount of net profit made from every £ of sales • Percentage of profit made on sales after expenses are deducted	3

Question			Expected answer(s)	Max mark
		ii	**Gross Profit has <u>decreased</u> possibly due to:**	3
			• Sales revenue has decreased, e.g. sales price has fallen/fewer customers purchasing • Wet summers reduce ice cream sales • Suppliers prices increasing • Economic recession • Competitive market	
			Profit For The Year has <u>decreased</u> in 2012 possibly due to:	
			• Wage costs may have risen • Marketing costs increased • Other income could have decreased	
			Profit For The Year has <u>increased</u> in 2013 possibly due to:	
			• Cheaper supplier • Cheaper/reduced energy • Less borrowing • Reduced wages • More automation • Cheaper advertising methods, e.g. social media	

SECTION 2

Question			Expected answer(s)	Max mark

2	a		• **Bonus/Performance-related pay** — an additional payment on top of a basic wage or salary which will be received when agreed targets are met
			• **Commission** — calculated as a percentage of sales value made by the employee and is added to a basic wage
			• **Piece rate** — when the employee is paid per item they produce
			  • Quality may be compromised if workers are rushing to increase output
			• **Overtime** — paid when an employee works longer than their contractual hours at a higher rate than their basic rate of pay
			• **Share-save schemes** — this is when employees save regular amounts each month for a set period after which their savings can be turned into shares in the business to be kept or sold at a profit
			• **Fringe benefits** — rewards offered to employees as well as their wage/salary, e.g. company car, discount, gym membership, etc.
			  • A company car can make the employee loyal to the firm/retain the worker
			
			Empowerment...
			Job enrichment...
			Promotion prospects...
			Good rate of pay...
			Good working conditions...
			Quality circle...
			Appraisal...
			Work council...
			Worker director...
			Positive corporate culture...
			Open door policy...
			Team working/building...
				4

	b		• Good practice can be acknowledged which motivates the employee • Good practice can be highlighted and shared with all employees within the organisation, which can then be followed by the other employees • Improvements to policies and procedures can be made due to feedback from staff • Training needs can be identified which can increase quality standards • The firm can ensure all employees are aware of the organisation's aims and are working towards achieving these • Strong relationships are formed between manager and employee as they are given the opportunity to have a professional discussion • Targets will be set for the employee which motivates them to be successful by giving them a goal to work towards • Wage increases and bonus can be linked to the appraisal system and administered as they are based on performance which can be viewed as a fairer system • Staff are highlighted for promotion which will retain a core workforce	4

Question			Expected answer(s)	Max mark
	c		• Gaps in the current staffing can be identified • Strategies can be put in place in order to fill gaps in staffing • Relevant training can be given • Staffing forecasts can be carried out • Allows continuity of production • Avoid overstaffing/surplus • Save costs through the use of outsourcing and sub-contracting • Flexible working practices may be considered so that staff are available when they are needed most • Workforce planning encourages managers to prepare and plan for changes rather than simply react to them • Allows businesses to prepare for periods of significant change, e.g. restructuring, technological change, growth, etc.	2
3	a		• No loss of control as the business is not integrating with others • Launch new products/services means businesses can target different markets • Exporting existing products abroad widens their market • Open new physical branches means they can reach new markets by opening up in new locations • Expand existing premises to cater for more products/staff and make more sales • Selling online the business can trade 24/7 around the world • Hire more staff will bring in new ideas to the business to develop new products/increase production, etc. • Increase production capacity by investing in new capital and technology to make more products themselves	4
	b		**Advantages** • Each division can meet the needs of local markets, e.g. different tastes or fashions in different towns or countries • The business can react to changing external (PESTEC) factors quickly • Easy to identify a failing division • Can hold divisional mangers accountable • Can communicate better with the local area, e.g. different languages **Disadvantages** • Duplication of resources, such as administration staff or IT equipment across each division • Divisions may compete against each other • A new division must established if a new area is targeted	3
	c		• Help tackle social problems it has chosen • Some funding/grants/support is only available to social enterprises • Publicity for the social issue promotes the business • Attract customers who appreciate the good causes they help • Attract good quality staff who want to help the social cause • Can make use of an asset lock • Can sell shares to raise finance if they are a limited company	3

4	a	i	• Cannot collude with other organisations to fix prices, e.g. cartel
			  • Cannot fix the bid for tendering on projects with other firms
			• Cannot use market power to pay unfairly low prices to suppliers
			• Prevents monopolies occurring
			  • Block mergers and take-overs that are deemed anti-competitive
			  • Enforcing the selling of divisions/branches/premises, e.g. divestment
			• May be forced change prices
			• May be fined for anti-competitive behaviour
				2

		ii	**Political** • Legislation and regulations will affect an organisation in that they need to comply with the laws **Economic** • Factors such as inflation, recession/boom periods, interest rates will affect organisations in a number of ways, i.e. consumers not spending as much on luxury items/more expensive to borrow money **Social** • Changes in trends and fashions mean that organisations must continually carry out market research **Technological** • As technology changes organisations must keep up-to-date and this will involve a large financial cost **Environmental** • Organisations now attempt to be socially responsible and environmentally friendly to possibly comply with legislation/satisfy consumer groups • Weather/flooding can mean a loss in sales if organisation cannot open due to flooding	5

Question			Expected answer(s)	Max mark
	b		• Tactical decisions are made to achieve the strategic objectives whereas an operational decision is made to ensure smooth running of the business on a daily basis • Tactical decisions are normally made by middle managers whereas operational decisions can be made by any level of management (most likely to be lower level) • Tactical decisions are more likely to be medium term whereas operational are day-to-day • Tactical decisions have a medium level of risk however operational decisions have little or no risk	3

5	a		• Performs "What if" scenarios, e.g. IF statement
			• Produces graphs and charts
			• Formulae calculations are carried out instantly and accurately
			   • Formulae are amended automatically when the spreadsheet is amended
			   • Formulae can be replicated
			• Easy to edit/amend
			• Conditionally format data
			• Can secure data with passwords
			• Can use templates for financial statements
				4

	b		• **Database** – can be used to sort large quantities of information on suppliers and customers
			• **Word Processor** – can be used to send letters and invoices to customers
			   • Preparing financial reports
			• **PowerPoint** – used to present information to staff
			• **Internet** – used to check share prices/exchange rates
			   • **Online banking** saves travelling to the bank
			• **Video-conferencing** – finance manager can hold meetings with other managers without leaving their office
			• **Email** – messages can be sent to more than one employee at a time
			• **Attachments** – can be sent to customers, e.g. invoices
			• **Network (LAN/4G/Cloud)** – can share files with all staff members
			• **Smartphone** – allows for teleworking/remote meetings
			   • **Apps** - allow for portable accounting software, e.g. Sage and Quickbooks
			
			Electronic Point Of Sales (EPOS)...
			Electronic Funds Transfer Points Of Sale (EFTPOS)...
				6

HIGHER BUSINESS MANAGEMENT
2017

SECTION 1

Question			Expected answer(s)	Max mark
1	a		Responses could include the following: • Mary's Meals aims to support a school feeding programme for children all over the world, whereas a public sector organisation aims to provide a service to a local/regional area. • Mary's Meals has an objective to maximise donations, whereas a public sector organisation has the objective to use public funds effectively. • Both Mary's Meals and a public sector organisation aim to provide the best service possible. • Both organisations aim to support education in the community. • Both organisations have the objective to be socially responsible. • Both organisations aim to support people in poverty. Accept any other suitable response.	3

	b		Responses could include the following:
			
			• It may be cheaper to import food/materials but this would create more pollution which could result in a poor image for the company.
			  • Importing goods would not support local business which could lower respect in the area.
			• Legislation differences may exist limiting the activities of Mary's Meals.
			  • It can be expensive to train staff in new legislation requirements.
			  • Quotas could be imposed limiting business activity.
			• Varied taxation and accounting requirements may be imposed between countries which could complicate financial transactions.
			• Cultural differences could result in the need to retrain staff or risk offending locals.
			• Working hours and conditions may vary which could result in HR issues for transferred staff.
			• Language barriers can exist making communication problematic.
			
			Accept any other suitable response.
				5

	c		Responses could include the following: • **Website** using text and images online to market to a global audience. • **Celebrity endorsement** such as Gerard Butler can raise awareness amongst fans. • **Animation** such as the Saving Grace story showing moving images and sound to convey information. • **Sponsorship** of a school will raise awareness at events in return for support. • **Stage work** such as film-making to raise awareness to a large audience. Accept any other suitable response.	5
	d		Responses could include the following: • Creates a positive image for the organisation which can allow them to attract high quality staff in the recruitment process. • May allow them to receive grants and incentives by complying with government policy. • More likely to receive donations and therefore increase funds. • A good reputation from good word of mouth will raise awareness of the organisation. • Help to achieve the company mission statement and objectives. Accept any other suitable response.	3

	e		Responses could include the following:
			
			• **Postal surveys** can be sent out to donors' homes and returned.
			  • Target an area at a relatively low cost.
			  • Low success rate as many people consider postal surveys as junk mail.
			• **Face-to-face interviews** provide instant feedback/clarification.
			  • Allows for body language/facial expressions to be seen which can improve communication.
			  • Can persuade people to donate more effectively if face-to-face.
			  • Poor interviewer/personality may intimidate.
			• **Customer/employee focus groups** give a range of opinions from a diverse group.
			  • May be expensive to run as often members need paid.
			• **Telephone surveys** often carried out by calling and asking questions remotely.
			  • Often seen as a nuisance and therefore may suffer for a low response rate.
			• Online survey...
			• Desk research...
			
			Accept any other suitable response.
				6

Question			Expected answer(s)	Max mark
f	i		Responses could include the following: • Due to an increase in promotional methods used by Mary's Meals. • A change of culture as society becomes more responsive to ethical businesses. • More disposable income in the economy. • An increase in fundraising and charitable events. • The website allows for donations to be made online. Accept any other suitable response.	2
	ii		Responses could include the following: • Donations do not have to be paid back unlike a bank loan which requires the amount to be repaid over time with interest. • Donations vary in amount unlike a bank loan which is a specified amount. • A bank loan can be requested up front at a far greater amount than donations for expansion purposes. • Donations may take longer to receive, whereas a bank loan could be delivered in full if terms are met. • Commercial mortgage is taken out against a property, whereas a bank overdraft is short-term access to finance which is expected to be paid off quickly. • Venture capital… • Government grant… • Hire purchase/leasing… Accept any other suitable response.	2
g			Responses could include the following: • An absence of volunteers/available staff could result in low productivity and fewer children being fed. • A lack of donations/funding or appropriate budgeting can result in reduced services. • Some volunteers/employees may lack skill which could lead to poor workmanship. • Managers may lack experience to launch projects successfully which can damage the organisation's reputation. • There may be a lack of information available leading to poor decision-making. • Poorly maintained technology could break down resulting in a halt in service. • Networks and company wifi availability allows its volunteers to stay better informed around the world. Accept any other suitable response.	4

SECTION 2

Question			Expected answer(s)	Max mark

2	a		Responses could include:
			
			• Through uniforms, staff will form an identity with the organisation which should result in lower staff turnover/absences
			  • Increased staff motivation because they feel part of the organisation/associate strongly with the culture
			• A single corporate identity is seen by customers which means they will then associate it with that organisation's brands/ethics/logos etc.
			  • Easily be recognised worldwide meaning customers will feel comfortable with products wherever they are
			• Values/beliefs/perks can attract quality staff which results in a better quality service
			• Customer satisfaction can improve because the customers begin to associate with the brands/logos/ethics they like
			  • Can attract new customers as they agree with the aims of the organisation
			  • Customers may become loyal...
			• Staff can move between branches/departments more easily as they will all be using the same policies and practices
			  • Workspace design/layout...
			  • Open door policy...
				3

	b		Responses could include:
			
			• Managers are in charge of more staff
			  • Managers can be placed under more stress
			  • Decision making can be slower due to a larger workload
			• Could result in less managerial promotions
			• Can mean managers have very little time to spend with each employee to discuss work
			  • Staff could become demotivated
			• It can be motivational for managers as they have more responsibility
			• Managers will have less time for planning
			  • May result in poor decisions
			• Managers can delegate to staff with appropriate skills
			  • Subordinates may resent additional responsibility
			  • Delegation can motivate/empower staff
				5

	c		Responses could include: • Employees are likely to want higher wages than the owners/managers are willing to pay • Owners/managers may need to reorganise the business but employees may feel this gives them extra responsibility without training or extra reward • Owners want to maintain control of their business but managers can become too powerful and influential through their decision making • Managers may focus on their objectives for financial reward which will conflict with owner's desire for maximum profit • Customers want delivery of goods as soon as possible but the managers cannot meet customer expectation because of the cost • Managers want to delay payment for goods bought to improve cash flow but suppliers want their money as soon as possible to avoid cash flow issues of their own	2
3	a		Responses could include: • Identifies best practice in the market therefore will improve the performance of the organisation if those techniques are adopted • It enhances competitiveness • It is a continuous process of striving to improve • Can be motivational for employees giving them goals to achieve • May identify other functions that could be improved • It can be difficult to gather all the relevant information needed as it is often not publicised • It can be time consuming to study and analyse competitors' techniques • Techniques may not be able to be adopted by the organisation due to internal constraints e.g. limited finance • Can only be as good as the benchmark set • Minimise the risk of the product failing when launched onto market	4

Question			Expected answer(s)	Max mark
	b		Responses could include: • Purchase recyclable materials • Reusing waste from the production line • Reduce carbon footprint • Minimise noise pollution created by the manufacturing process • Use sustainable energy e.g. install solar panels or build a wind farm • Use less packaging of products	3
	c		Responses could include: • Products are unique • Made to suit customers' requirements • Higher prices can be charged • The product can be altered during production process • Seeing a job through can be motivating for employees • Highly skilled workers make quality products	3

4	a		Responses could include:
			
			• It shows whether the business will have a surplus of cash which will allow them to plan future purchases
			• It shows whether the business will have a deficit which will allow them to make adjustments to spending
			  • Or arrange an injection of cash to avoid the deficit
			• To make comparisons between predicted and actual figures this will help monitor the performance of the business
			• Highlighting periods where expenses may be high will allow action to be taken to control spending
			• It aids decision making as it provides cash flow information for decisions to be based on
			• It can be used to set targets for individual departments to achieve which will allow the business to stay within budget as predicted
			  • Targets set can also help motivate employees as they have goals to work towards
			• It can empower employees as each department can be set a budget which will give department managers responsibility of spending and recording their finances
				5

	b		Responses could include: • Inability to pay suppliers • Raw materials may not be supplied • Unable to pay expenses • May need to find a cheaper supplier • May have to offer discounts to encourage customers on credit to pay early • Increased costs due to borrowing funds i.e. interest and bank charges • Lack of disposable funds to invest e.g. to purchase new technology • Low employee morale due to pressure to increase sales revenue • Restricted growth as there is no funds to invest in and support growing the businesses operations • Owner may need to reduce their drawings • May need to sell unused assets • May need to reduce prices of goods • Might lead to staff redundancies • Solvency risk/closure/administration	5
5	a		Responses could include: • Allows employees to make decisions once they have been given a task • Employees are expected to solve problems on their own with very little guidance from the group leader • Leaders only step in if they are needed/asked • Laissez-faire leadership can be effective in situations where employees are highly skilled, motivated, and capable of working on their own • Inexperienced staff will not be given much direction/support • Could result in poor quality of work • Employees may feel more pressure and become stressed	3

Question			Expected answer(s)	Max mark

	b		Responses could include:
			
			Equality Act
			• The organisation may be prosecuted for discrimination eg fine
			• Employers may have to revise their recruitment policies
			• Pay both genders the same for jobs of equal value
			• Wording in job adverts must not be discriminatory
			• Invest in better accessibility e.g. installing lifts, ramps, etc.
			• Investigate issues of discrimination/harassment/victimisation against an employee, customer or a third party
			• Train staff on discrimination prevention/awareness
			
			National Minimum Wage Act
			• An increase in minimum wage leads to increased costs for the organisation
			  • This could result in lowered profits as wage expenses increase
			• If it is found that an organisation has not been paying the minimum wage, they may be required to make a backdated payment for employees
			
			Health and Safety at Work Act
			• Must provide the correct safety equipment
			• Could be temporarily closed or shut down for non-compliance
			• Potential for legal action by members of staff if they suffer injury at work due to non-compliance
			  • This may result in compensation payments
			
			Employment Rights Act
			• Issue employees with payslips
			• Must have a written disciplinary policy in place if over a certain size
			• May be time consuming and costly to implement/update policies and procedures
			• Must issue employees with a contract after a certain period of time
			
			Data Protection Act...
				4

	c		Responses could include:
			
			• Employees may become a registered member of a professional institute
			  • Can increase salary when qualified
			• Employees can be awarded "in-house" certificates once training has been completed
			• Employees may have better chance of promotion after training as training is relevant to the job
			  • However, may leave for a better paid job after gaining qualification
			• Training can be logged in their CPD record to comply with minimum training standards/contracted development time
			• Work-based qualification can be tailored to suit the firm's needs
			• Training normally takes place in the workplace which can save costs for the organisation
			• Can be time consuming as it could be done on a part-time basis
			• Can be costly to pay for the trainers
				3

Acknowledgements

Permission has been sought from all relevant copyright holders and Hodder Gibson is grateful for the use of the following:

Information has been adapted from pages 4–25 of J Sainsbury plc Annual Report and Financial Statements 2013. Reproduced by kind permission of J Sainsbury plc (SQP pages 2–5);
Sainsbury's market share — 'Kantar Worldpanel total till roll for the 52 weeks to 17 March 2013' is reproduced by kind permission of Kantar Worldpanel (SQP page 4);
A photograph, extract and logos for Google © Google PLC (2015 pages 2–5);
Image © Twin Design/Shutterstock.com (2015 page 3);
Extracts and images reproduced by permission of Mackie's of Scotland (2016 pages 2–5);
Image supplied courtesy of 'The Scottish Farmer' © Newsquest (Herald & Times) Ltd. (2016 page 4);
Statistics from Companies House (https://beta.companieshouse.gov.uk/company/SC030096/filing-history).
Contains public sector information licensed under the Open Government Licence v3.0
(https://www.nationalarchives.gov.uk/doc/open-government-licence/version/3/) (2016 page 6);
Logo and extracts taken from http://www.marysmeals.org.uk. Reproduced by permission of Mary's Meals (2017 pages 2–5).